UNDERSTANDING YOUR WOMAN

A self help guide for men and women

While every precaution has been taken in the preparation of this book, the publisher assumes no responsibility for errors or omissions, or for damages resulting from the use of the information contained herein.

UNDERSTANDING YOUR WOMAN

Table of Contents

This book is dedicated to the women in my life that have played a significant roles forging me into the man I am today and to my aunt Annie Young who has always been there pushing me when I wanted to give up. I love you auntie!

PREFACE

Welcome to "Understanding Your Woman: A Self-Help Guide." In a world filled with diverse and intricate relationships, understanding the complexities of the women we cherish is a journey worth embarking upon. This book aims to provide you with valuable insights, practical advice, and effective strategies to enhance your understanding of the women in your life, whether it be your partner, wife, girlfriend, friend, or family member.

The dynamics of relationships have evolved over time, and so have our expectations of each other. As we strive for equality and mutual respect, it becomes essential to embrace the uniqueness of every individual, recognizing that women, like men, have multifaceted dimensions that deserve appreciation and comprehension.

This guide is not about perpetuating stereotypes or generalizations; rather, it is an invitation to delve into the depths of human emotion, communication, and connection. Our intention is to foster empathy, compassion, and growth, enabling stronger bonds and more fulfilling relationships.

Throughout this journey, we will explore the intricacies of effective communication, emotional intelligence, and the art of empathetic listening. We will discuss the significance of recognizing and respecting the diverse needs of the women in our lives and how to navigate the ever-changing tides of emotions with understanding and grace.

"Understanding Your Woman: A Self-Help Guide" goes beyond simply unraveling the mysteries of women—it is an exploration of love, trust, intimacy, and support. It is about empowering women to be their authentic selves and encouraging men to be their best partners. By nurturing these connections, we can create a harmonious and loving environment where both partners thrive.

As you read through these pages, we encourage you to approach each topic with an open mind and a willingness to learn. Acknowledge that everyone's experiences are unique, and there is no one-size-fits-all approach to understanding the women in our lives. Instead, let this guide serve as a starting point for conversations, reflections, and growth in your relationships.

Remember that understanding is an ongoing process, and as you embark on this journey, you may discover new dimensions to the women you love and care for. Embrace the challenges and celebrate the triumphs that come with nurturing meaningful connections.

May this guide be a beacon of guidance and inspiration, illuminating the path to a deeper appreciation and understanding of the women in your life. We hope that by the end of this book, you will not only gain valuable insights but also forge stronger and more meaningful bonds with the women who hold a special place in your heart.

With sincerity and utmost respect for the essence of human relationships,

CALVIN BROWN SR.

Chapter 1 Introduction

In this chapter, we delve into the significance of the woman in your life, whether she is your partner, spouse, mother, sister, or friend. We will explore the unique qualities and contributions she brings to your life, the profound impact she has on your emotional well-being, and the importance of cherishing and supporting her in return. Recognizing and understanding the value of the women in our lives is essential for fostering meaningful relationships and creating a harmonious world.

Chapter 1.1 Why Understanding Your Woman is Important

Understanding your woman goes beyond surface-level comprehension; it delves into the depths of her emotions, needs, and aspirations. In a world where gender roles are evolving, fostering a genuine understanding of the women in our lives is more crucial than ever. By recognizing the significance of this endeavor, we can build stronger relationships, promote gender equality, and empower women to reach their full potential. In this article, we will explore the reasons why understanding your woman is essential and how it positively impacts both individuals and society.

Effective communication is the cornerstone of any healthy relationship. When you take the time to understand your woman's communication style, feelings, and perspectives, you pave the way for a deeper emotional connection. By being attentive and empathetic, you can create an environment where she feels comfortable expressing herself openly, strengthening the bond between you both.

Understanding your woman is not only about listening but also about acknowledging her experiences, opinions, and ideas. Women have long been marginalized and silenced in various aspects of life. By valuing her voice and actively supporting her endeavors, you contribute to empowering women and promoting gender equality.

Each woman has her unique dreams and aspirations, whether in her career, personal life, or hobbies. When you make the effort to understand her passions and ambitions, you can become a supportive partner, helping her achieve her goals and nurturing her personal growth. This support not only benefits her but also strengthens the foundation of your relationship.

Understanding your woman is crucial for maintaining a healthy, balanced and fulfilling relationship. It moves beyond mere appreciation of her personality, and delves into recognizing her needs, feelings, preferences, and unique qualities. It's about learning her communication style, knowing when to provide space or when to lend a supportive shoulder. Understanding your woman fosters deep emotional connection, trust, and mutual respect. It can strengthen the bond between you, improve your ability to resolve conflicts, and enhance your overall relationship satisfaction. Every woman is unique with her own set of desires, fears, hopes and dreams. Thus, understanding your woman is a continuous, rewarding journey of discovery that stems from effective communication, empathy, patience, and love.

Chapter 1.2 Misconceptions and Stereotypes

Misconceptions and stereotypes about women have been prevalent throughout history and continue to exist in various cultures and societies. These misconceptions and stereotypes can be harmful as they contribute to gender inequality and limit women's opportunities and potential. Here are some common examples of misconceptions and stereotypes about women:

One of the common stereotypes is that women are more emotional and less rational than men. This belief can lead to women being perceived as overly sensitive or incapable of making logical decisions, which can undermine their abilities in both personal and professional settings.

One stereotype suggests that a woman's primary role is to be a caregiver and homemaker, while her career should take a backseat. It can lead to societal pressure on women to choose between family and career, limiting their choices and opportunities.

It is essential to challenge these misconceptions and stereotypes about women and promote gender equality. Encouraging education and awareness, providing equal opportunities in education and the workforce, and supporting policies that address gender bias can help dismantle these harmful beliefs and create a more inclusive and equal society for all genders. Additionally, celebrating and valuing diversity and promoting women's achievements and contributions can help challenge and break down these stereotypes over time.

Women often face a myriad of misconceptions and stereotypes, which can lead to gender bias and discrimination. One prevalent stereotype is the notion that women are not as logical or analytical as men, a misconception that is especially harmful in fields like science, technology, engineering, and mathematics. This stereotype is challenged by the numerous accomplished women in these fields. Another stereotype is the assumption that women are inherently more nurturing and suited for caring roles. This creates a bias that often limits women's career choices and undermines their contributions in other fields. It is crucial to challenge and dismiss such misconceptions to foster gender equality.

In the workplace, addressing gender bias is essential to creating an equitable environment for both men and women. Employers should be aware of potential unconscious biases that may arise in hiring processes, job promotions, or in assigning roles and responsibilities. It is also important to address stereotypes regarding women's leadership capabilities, such as the notion that women are less decisive or lack assertiveness. By recognizing and eliminating such biases, organizations can foster an environment where everyone is valued for their skills and contributions.

Further, it is important to ensure that policies are in place to promote gender equality. This includes measures like ensuring equal pay for equal work, providing adequate parental leave benefits, and ensuring flexible working hours. Such policies help to create a supportive environment that allows both men and women to be successful in their careers.

Ultimately, gender bias and discrimination should not receive any tolerance or acceptance, whether it is in the workplace, school, or any other setting. It is important to recognize that everyone has value regardless of their gender identity or expression. By standing together and challenging these biases, we can create a more equitable society for all.

Chapter 1.3 How This Guide Can Help You

"Understanding Your Woman: A Self-Help Guide" is designed to be your compass in navigating the intricate terrain of relationships with the women in your life. This guide offers practical insights, actionable advice, and valuable strategies to enrich your understanding and strengthen your connections. Here's how this guide can benefit you:

- Enhancing Empathy and Communication: By exploring the principles of emotional intelligence and effective communication, you will learn how to empathize with your woman's emotions and perspectives. Understanding her unique communication style and emotional needs will enable you to respond with greater sensitivity and clarity, minimizing misunderstandings and conflicts.

- Unraveling Complexity: Women, like all individuals, possess multifaceted dimensions. This guide helps you embrace the complexity of the women in your life by encouraging you to appreciate their individuality and uniqueness. You will learn to approach each woman with an open mind and a willingness to understand her as a whole person, free from stereotypes or assumptions.

- Nurturing Emotional Intimacy: The journey to understanding your woman is a pathway to fostering emotional intimacy. By learning to listen actively, express empathy, and support her emotional well-being, you will create a profound and meaningful connection that enriches your relationship.

- Balancing Independence and Togetherness: Understanding your woman involves supporting her personal growth and ambitions while cultivating a strong partnership. This guide provides insights into nurturing independence while maintaining a sense of togetherness, creating a harmonious and fulfilling relationship dynamic.

- Conflict Resolution and Healthy Disagreements: Conflict is an inevitable part of any relationship. This guide equips you with conflict resolution strategies that encourage open dialogue, mutual respect, and collaboration. You will learn how to navigate disagreements constructively, strengthening the bond with your woman through challenges.

- Discovering Love Languages: Every individual has unique preferences for giving and receiving love. This guide introduces the concept of love languages and helps you identify your woman's primary love language, enabling you to express affection and appreciation in ways that resonate deeply with her.

- Supporting Her Well-Being: Understanding your woman's emotional needs, experiences, and challenges enables you to provide meaningful support and encouragement. This guide emphasizes the importance of being a compassionate and caring partner, empowering her to thrive in all aspects of life.

- Breaking Free from Stereotypes: By encouraging you to see your woman as an individual with her own dreams and aspirations, this guide challenges harmful stereotypes and misconceptions. You will learn to appreciate her strengths and contributions, fostering an environment of equality and respect.

- Cultivating Gratitude and Fulfillment: As you deepen your understanding of the women in your life, you will find new opportunities for gratitude and appreciation. This guide inspires you to celebrate her successes, cherish her presence, and find fulfillment in nurturing meaningful connections.
- Building Lasting Relationships: Ultimately, this guide aims to strengthen your relationships with the women you care about, be it a romantic partner, family member, or friend. By incorporating the principles outlined in this guide, you can build lasting and meaningful relationships grounded in empathy, respect, and love.

Let this guide be your companion on the journey to understanding your woman. Embrace the wisdom it offers, and with an open heart and a commitment to growth, you will lay the foundation for enriching and rewarding relationships that stand the test of time.

Chapter 2 The Complexity of Women

Women, like all humans, embody a beautiful complexity that should not be oversimplified. Their experiences, shaped by their identities, backgrounds, and societal structures, are diverse and multifaceted. They juggle multiple roles, often navigating the overlapping spheres of professional, personal, and societal expectations with grace and resilience. This complexity is a vital part of their strength, contributing to the richness and diversity of human experience.

Despite this complexity, women often face unique challenges, some of which are rooted in gender-based discrimination and inequalities. These include economic disparities, lack of representation in leadership roles, and an increased burden of unpaid labor. Additionally, women experience higher levels of violence than their male peers and are disproportionately affected by poverty. These issues have been compounded by the current global pandemic, which has impacted women's economic security and well-being in disproportionate ways.

In order to address these issues, it is essential to understand how they manifest in different contexts and what strategies can be utilized to combat them. This includes addressing structural and cultural barriers that impede gender equity, promoting the inclusion of diverse perspectives in decision-making processes, and investing in initiatives that promote economic security for women.

At the same time, it is important to recognize and celebrate the strength, resilience, and achievements of women around the world. This includes recognizing their contributions to science, arts, civil society movements, as well as their role in nurturing our communities. By supporting one another and creating safe spaces to foster meaningful connections, women are ensuring that their voices are heard and that our society moves towards a more inclusive future.

It is also essential to listen to the experiences of marginalized communities, including those who identify as LGBTQIA2+, Indigenous, racialized or living with disabilities. These individuals often face multiple layers of discrimination and marginalization, and it is important to ensure that they have access to adequate services, resources and support. This includes amplifying their stories, recognizing their unique needs and advocating for the improvement of their rights and representation.

Finally, it is important to recognize that gender equality cannot be achieved without dismantling existing systems of oppression. This requires challenging dominant narratives that perpetuate inequality, engaging in transformative dialogue around difficult topics such as patriarchy and racism, and creating inclusive environments where everyone is respected and celebrated. Moreover, it involves committing to learning about our own biases and privilege, in order to become better allies for the advancement of gender justice. By working together towards a more equitable society, we can ensure that all people have access to the same rights and opportunities regardless of their gender identity or expression. Together, we can create a world where everyone is respected and valued.

By engaging in dialogue, we can create a space to examine our own beliefs and values, question oppressive systems, and build meaningful connections with one another. We must remember that progress towards gender equality is an ongoing process, requiring us to stay informed and active in order to make lasting change. It is essential to listen to different voices and perspectives, acknowledge our differences, and strive for greater understanding. As we move forward in this journey towards justice and equality, we must come together to celebrate our shared humanity and do our part in creating a more equitable society.

We cannot achieve gender parity without collective action. We must work together to advocate for change, challenge the status quo, and ensure that everyone has access to the same rights and opportunities regardless of their gender identity or expression. From creating positive media representations of diverse genders and identities, to challenging stereotypes in our day-to-day lives, it is important for us all to play a role in dismantling oppressive structures. Only through collective action can we create an environment where everyone feels respected and included.

We must also continue to support and uplift marginalized voices. In particular, we should work to center the experiences of trans individuals who are too often silenced or excluded from public discourse about gender equality. Only by listening to and learning from these voices can we create a world where everyone is free to express their true selves without fear or discrimination.

It is also important to recognize that gender equality is not a singular issue. Rather, it is intertwined with issues of race and class, and affects everyone differently depending on their individual identity. We must be aware of the ways in which systemic injustice intersects with gender inequality and strive to create solutions that address all these disparities at once.

By recognizing our shared commitment to gender equality, we can start to create a better world for everyone. Together, let us continue to work towards justice and equity in our communities. Let us strive to create a society where all genders are respected and where everyone is afforded the same rights and opportunities regardless of who they are or who they love. Our collective efforts will be key to achieving true gender parity worldwide.

It's not enough to simply talk about gender equality: we must take action. From resisting gender-based discrimination in hiring and promotions, to creating safe spaces for people of all genders, to advocating for laws that promote gender equity, there are countless ways we can work to advance equality. Let us stand together and commit ourselves to taking these steps so that our world becomes a more just and inclusive place. Together, we can create a future where everyone is respected, valued, and free from oppression.

Let us also remember that everyone has a role to play in creating a more equitable future. From pushing for better media and cultural It is our responsibility to ensure that all genders are treated equally, with dignity and respect. We must challenge the status quo and call out sexism and misogyny whenever we encounter it. We must also recognize the unique challenges that people of all genders face, and work towards solutions that empower them to thrive and live accord gender representation to creating more equitable economic opportunities, there are many ways you can make a difference in the fight for gender equality.

Chapter 2.1 Embracing Individual Differences

Embracing individual differences in women is a critical principle that shapes the dynamics of society at large. Each woman, with her unique blend of experiences, skills, cultural background, and perspectives, adds a distinct flavor to the societal fabric. Recognizing and honoring these differences can lead to expanded understanding and appreciation of diversity, ultimately fostering an environment that encourages personal growth and community enrichment. Valuing individual differences also sets the stage for stronger bonds, enhanced collaboration, and the propagation of enriched ideas that can spur innovation and social progress.

By understanding the power of individual differences, we can create a space for meaningful dialogue and exchange of ideas. This is important for creating an atmosphere that fosters creativity and encourages diverse perspectives to be shared. Additionally, it can lead to deeper empathy and insight into the lives of others, which helps in fostering greater personal connection and mutual respect. Such an environment can lead to more inclusive and understanding social interactions, thus promoting broader acceptance of individual differences throughout society.

Moreover, it is essential to recognize that individual differences are not only limited to gender but can also encompass race, ethnicity, sexual orientation, economic background, physical ability/disability status, age and religion. Allowing for the expression of multiple identities can help create a space of acceptance and understanding for everyone, while at the same time inspiring greater collaboration and innovation.

Ultimately, it is essential to recognize that individual differences are what make us unique and can help bring about social progress. By embracing a culture of inclusion, we can create an environment where every person's voice is heard and respected. Valuing individual differences ultimately leads to a more vibrant and collaborative society where everyone can find their place.

At the same time, it is important to remember that individual differences should always be celebrated in an appropriate manner that respects the dignity of every person. This means taking care to avoid stereotypes and discriminatory language, as well as avoiding making assumptions about another person's beliefs or background. Ultimately, by embracing individual differences we can create a society that is both diverse and united.

In order to promote such an environment, it is important for organizations to commit themselves to valuing diversity. This could include recruiting people from a variety of backgrounds and providing them with equal opportunities for promotion and growth. It may also involve creating policies that discourage discrimination and address any grievances raised by employees. Finally, it is important to ensure that everyone in the workplace feels respected and safe so that they can contribute their unique perspectives and talents without fear of judgement or reprisal.

By recognizing individual differences and embracing diversity, businesses can create a more productive and innovative environment that encourages collaboration and inspires creativity. Such an attitude will not only benefit the organization itself, but will also help to create a more equitable and inclusive society. This, in turn, will benefit us all.

In conclusion, valuing individual differences is essential for creating a more compassionate and unified society. Organizations should strive to create an environment that celebrates diversity and allows everyone to share their unique gifts and perspectives. By doing so, we can create a brighter future where every voice matters.

It is also essential to ensure that everyone is treated with respect. This means avoiding offensive language and stereotypes. It is also important for each of us as individuals to be open and accepting of those who are different from us. We should strive to treat others with kindness and understanding, abstaining from prejudicial attitudes respecting diversity also encourages greater acceptance and understanding among people of diverse backgrounds and cultures.

It encourages openness to new ideas and promotes greater collaboration between people from all walks of life. This, in turn, can lead to innovative solutions that benefit everyone. No matter who we are or where we come from, we all have something unique and valuable to contribute to the world. By recognizing this fundamental truth and creating a culture of respect and understanding, we can create a better future for us all.

Chapter 2.2 Emotional Intelligence

Women often display high levels of emotional intelligence, thereby contributing significantly to their personal and professional relationships. Emotional intelligence, defined as the ability to understand, use, and manage one's own emotions in positive ways, is frequently seen in women's ability to empathize, communicate effectively, overcome challenges, and defuse conflict. It's a trait that not only enhances interpersonal interactions but also optimizes decision-making processes, creating a harmonious and productive environment.

Women's emotional intelligence can also serve as an invaluable asset in the business world, where it can be used to help companies foster better relationships with customers, build strong teams, and cultivate a positive organizational culture.

Overall, women's emotional intelligence is a powerful tool which can be utilized to create meaningful change within organizations and communities. By recognizing the unique value that women bring to the table, companies can produce more innovative solutions and foster a culture of collaboration and growth. Additionally, when women's emotional intelligence is taken into account in policy-making decisions, it can lead to better outcomes for everyone involved. In this way, women's emotional intelligence can be an invaluable resource for creating stronger societies.

In order to truly benefit from the power of emotional intelligence, however, it is essential that women receive the support and recognition they need from their peers, employers, and society as a whole. This means providing them with the necessary resources to develop their skills and offering opportunities for advancement in all aspects of life. Furthermore, ensuring that women are not discriminated against or subjected to unfair treatment due to their gender is also a key component in achieving equality and recognizing the value of their emotional intelligence.

By investing in women's emotional intelligence, organizations can reap numerous rewards such as improved communication, better problem-solving skills, increased collaboration, enhanced customer loyalty, and higher levels of employee satisfaction. Additionally, when women are given a seat at the table and respected for their contributions to business, it can be a catalyst for greater creativity and innovation. In this way, emotional intelligence can be a powerful tool for positively transforming organizations and making a real impact on communities.

At the same time, men should also be encouraged to develop their emotional intelligence in order to better recognize and respond to the emotions of those around them. By improving their own emotional intelligence, men can become better allies for women in the workplace and make an integral contribution towards creating an environment where everyone can feel

The importance of fostering emotional intelligence in young girls should not be underestimated as it lays the foundation for success in adulthood. Providing girls with the tools and resources to recognize, understand, and manage their own emotions is an essential part of creating a more equitable society. Furthermore, teaching girls how to empathize with others and build positive relationships can help them navigate challenging situations in work and life. Ultimately, developing emotional intelligence among young women can lead to greater resilience in the face of adversity as well as increased self-confidence, allowing them to take on more meaningful roles in their personal and professional lives.

By creating programs that focus on the development of emotional intelligence among women and men alike, we can help bridge the gender gap in today's society and create a better future for everyone. By recognizing the power of emotional intelligence as an essential tool for personal and professional success, we can create a more equitable society where everyone has a chance at achieving their goals.

As the saying goes, "knowledge is power" and emotional intelligence can be the key to unlocking that power. By empowering women to recognize and use their emotions effectively, they can become strong voices for change in their communities.

Finally, when women are empowered to use their emotional intelligence effectively, they become more confident in their abilities and better prepared to take on leadership roles in all aspects of life. This can help to further promote gender equality, bolster economic growth, and create a more inclusive and equitable society. By recognizing the power of emotional intelligence and providing women with the necessary resources to develop their skills, we can all benefit from a brighter future.

2.3 Navigating Hormonal Changes

Hormonal changes in women can often feel like navigating through stormy seas, with fluctuations causing a myriad of physical and emotional symptoms. From puberty to pregnancy, and then menopause, these hormone shifts are a natural part of a woman's life cycle. Understanding these changes is the first step to managing them effectively. Lifestyle modifications, including a balanced diet, regular exercise, stress management techniques, and adequate sleep, can have a significant impact in maintaining hormonal balance. Furthermore, consulting with healthcare professionals can provide tailored advice and treatment options.

A key component to managing the symptoms of hormone fluctuations is knowledge and understanding. With this comes the ability to make informed lifestyle decisions, as well as being able to identify when medical assistance may be needed. Endeavoring to stay educated about hormones can help manage any imbalances and maximize overall health and wellbeing.

Women are not alone in experiencing hormonal changes; men too can have their hormones affected by lifestyle factors such as stress and diet. The shift in hormones can result in a range of physical and emotional symptoms, including fatigue, poor concentration levels, depression, irritability and weight gain. Although these signs may be subtle at first, addressing them early on is important to avoid long-term issues. For men, much like women, lifestyle modifications such as regular exercise, healthy eating and stress management can help to regulate hormone levels. Additionally, seeking medical advice may be beneficial to identify any underlying issues and establish a plan of action.

Overall, understanding the hormones in our body is essential for maintaining both physical and mental health. Educating ourselves on the impact hormones have on our lives can empower us to make healthier lifestyle choices and prevent any further imbalances. With the right information, tools and support, everyone has the potential to lead happier and more balanced lives.

Taking steps to recognize our own individual hormonal patterns can be beneficial to understanding how it affects each of us on a personal level. This awareness may provide insight into which aspects of our daily routines or habits may be impacting our hormones and subsequently allowing us to make informed decisions surrounding lifestyle modifications as needed. Seeking guidance from a healthcare professional can also be beneficial in order to gain assistance with formulating individualized plans for diet, exercise and other lifestsyle changes that may help to balance hormone levels. Taking the time to regularly check in with ourselves and assess how we are feeling can also help us to better identify any potential signs of hormonal imbalance. Common symptoms include fatigue, poor sleep quality, mood swings, cravings for sugar or carbs, headaches and dizziness.

It is important to remember that while hormones are largely responsible for our physical and mental health, nutrition and lifestyle habits play a major role in hormone regulation as well. Eating a diet rich in fruits, vegetables and whole grains as well as limiting processed foods can go a long way in maintaining hormone balance. Getting enough sleep and engaging in regular exercise are also important elements to consider when attempting to keep hormones regulated. Overall, it is essential to create an environment conducive for hormonal balance through both dietary and lifestyle changes. With the right information and support system, anyone can take control of their hormones and improve their overall health.

Avoiding exposure to environmental toxins is another way to support hormone health. Common sources of toxins include household cleaning products, cosmetics, air fresheners, pesticides and plastic packages for food. Whenever possible it is best to opt for natural options when shopping for these items and limit direct contact with materials that may contain toxins. Additionally, it is important to drink plenty of filtered water and make sure to get enough fiber in our diets, which can help flush out any potentially harmful substances that we are exposed to.

Taking certain supplements can also be beneficial in regulating hormones. Commonly used supplements include omega-3 fatty acids, magnesium, probiotics and vitamin D. It is important to speak with a healthcare provider before taking any supplement or altering your diet in order to ensure that it is right for you and your individual needs.

Making positive changes to our diets and lifestyle can have a profound impact on the health of our hormonal systems. By understanding how different foods and activities affect hormone production, we can create an environment that is conducive to balanced hormones and optimal well-being.

There are other therapies that may be beneficial in supporting hormone health as well. Herbal remedies such as red clover, maca, dong quai, chasteberry and ashwagandha have all been used traditionally to help balance hormones. Acupuncture and yoga may also be helpful in promoting relaxation and reducing stress, which can in turn help with regulating hormones. Additionally, getting plenty of restful sleep is key for overall health and maintaining hormone balance. Finally, engaging in regular physical activity can support hormonal health by reducing inflammation, regulating metabolic processes and improving mood.

Chapter 3 Effective Communication

Effective communication with women, like any other gender, involves empathy, respect, and understanding. It's crucial to listen actively, respect boundaries, and validate feelings and experiences. Discussions should be inclusive, acknowledging and respecting different perspectives and experiences. Remember, open-mindedness, patience, and a genuine interest in understanding others' worldviews pave the way for effective communication.

When talking to women, it's also important to create a safe and comfortable space. This means being aware of nonverbal communication—your tone and body language can be just as important as what you say. Further, try to avoid making assumptions about someone based on their gender or other factors like age or ethnicity. Embrace diversity and recognize that everyone's experiences are unique.

When it comes to difficult conversations, it is often helpful to take a few moments to compose yourself and be mindful of your own thoughts and feelings. Self-awareness can help you stay calm in tense situations and make sure the conversation remains respectful and productive. Additionally, if emotions become too overwhelming, it may be necessary to take a break from the conversation altogether. Taking a pause is perfectly fine and can help both parties communicate more effectively.

Although it can be uncomfortable, it's important to stay open to feedback if you make a mistake or misstep. Apologize sincerely, reflect on your behavior, and try to grow from the experience. And if someone else has wronged you, have honest conversations about it with patience and empathy. Ultimately, communication is key to building strong relationships with everyone you interact with, especially women. The more you practice active listening, the better your conversations will become.

It is also important to keep an open mind. Don't be afraid to question your own beliefs and values, or those of others. Ask questions, listen closely, and try to see things from different perspectives. This can help you better understand the people around you and foster a more inclusive environment. Above all else, be kind and respectful in every conversation—even when things get challenging. This is the best way to create a safe space for meaningful dialogue and mutual understanding.

Remember that communication is a two-way street—if the other person isn't comfortable discussing something, try to find common ground and focus on what you both agree upon. This can help to build trust and understanding in a respectful manner. Additionally, be aware of cultural nuances when speaking with people from different backgrounds. Everyone has different ways of expressing themselves, and it's important to be mindful of these nuances in order to create a positive and productive dialogue.

Finally, practice self-care and don't forget to take breaks when needed. Communication can be draining both mentally and emotionally, so it's important to give yourself time for reflection and relaxation. This will help ensure that your conversations are productive, meaningful, and leave both parties feeling heard and respected. With a little bit of effort, you can build strong relationships and create meaningful connections with the people around you.

Chapter 3.1 Active Listening Techniques

Active listening is an essential skill in effective communication. It involves not just hearing the words someone is saying but also understanding, interpreting, and responding thoughtfully to their message. Here are some active listening techniques to help you become a better listener:

- **Maintain Eye Contact**: Look at the speaker and maintain appropriate eye contact. It shows that you are engaged and interested in what they are saying.
- **Give Non-Verbal Cues**: Nodding your head, smiling, or using facial expressions to show understanding and encouragement can help the speaker feel supported.
- **Avoid Interrupting**: Allow the speaker to finish their thoughts before responding or asking questions. Interrupting can be disruptive and make the speaker feel disregarded.
- **Avoid Distractions**: Focus solely on the conversation and eliminate distractions, such as checking your phone or looking around the room.
- **Paraphrase**: Summarize or repeat what the speaker said in your own words. This technique confirms your understanding and lets the speaker know that you are paying attention.
- **Ask Open-Ended Questions**: Encourage the speaker to elaborate by asking open-ended questions like "Could you tell me more about that?" or "How did that make you feel?"

- **Reflect Emotions**: Pay attention to the speaker's emotions and reflect them back, saying things like, "It sounds like you felt really excited about that."
- **Empathize**: Show empathy and understanding by acknowledging the speaker's feelings or experiences. This can create a sense of connection and trust.
- **Avoid Judgments**: Refrain from making judgments or assumptions while listening. Be open-minded and consider the speaker's perspective.
- **Avoid Offering Immediate Solutions**: Sometimes, people just want to be heard and understood. Avoid jumping into problem-solving mode right away, unless the speaker specifically asks for advice.
- **Use Mirroring**: Repeat a few keywords or phrases the speaker used. It shows that you are actively following their thoughts.
- **Stay Neutral**: Be aware of your own biases and opinions. Maintain a neutral stance during the conversation.
- **Be Patient**: Some people take more time to express themselves. Be patient and give them the space they need.
- **Acknowledge Silence**: Don't rush to fill moments of silence. Sometimes, the speaker may need time to gather their thoughts.
- **Show Genuine Interest**: Be genuinely interested in what the speaker has to say, even if the topic isn't something you're passionate about.

By practicing these active listening techniques, you can improve your communication skills, strengthen relationships, and foster better understanding with others.

Active listening is a critical communication skill that requires full attention to the speaker and an understanding of the speaker's body language. It involves both hearing the words and understanding the message behind them, allowing for more effective communication. Active listening aids in understanding complex ideas, resolving conflicts, and building trust, making it an essential tool in both personal and professional interactions.

When engaging in active listening, it is important to maintain an open and non-judgmental attitude. Listeners should be patient and allow the speaker to fully express their thoughts without interruption. It can be helpful to paraphrase or summarize what was said to ensure that you have correctly understood the message; this also helps encourage further discussion as the speaker may be more willing to open up if they feel their ideas are being heard.

In addition, good active listeners use a variety of nonverbal cues to show that they understand and empathize with the speaker. These may include nodding in agreement, maintaining eye contact, or smiling to show interest or understanding. Such behaviors demonstrate an attentiveness which can encourage further dialogue on difficult topics.

Active listening is a skill that can take time to perfect, but the rewards are worth it. Developing and practicing this skill sets us up for better communication with those around us, which in turn can lead to more meaningful relationships and an improved sense of connection. Taking the time to actively listen shows respect for the speaker and helps create a stronger bond between people. Ultimately, active listening is an invaluable tool to anyone seeking to build relationships and foster effective communication.

Chapter 3.2 Non-Verbal Cues and Body Language

In interpersonal communication, non-verbal cues and body language often play a significant role, especially amongst women. Women tend to be more expressive and detailed with their gestures, using body language to communicate their feelings, ideas, and responses. For example, crossed arms might indicate defensiveness or closed-off attitudes. A warm, genuine smile can signal friendliness and openness, while minimal eye contact might hint at discomfort or disinterest. Understanding these cues is key to effective communication and building strong relationships.

Studies have also found that body language is particularly influential in the workplace. Women who express themselves with confidence and clarity are more likely to be taken seriously, whereas those who shy away from eye contact or avoid certain topics may not command as much respect. As such, proper body language can be an important tool for career advancement. It can also help create a secure and safe environment for constructive criticism, as non-verbal cues can help establish trust between colleagues. Moreover, body language is a powerful way to show appreciation for others' work and efforts. A nod or smile of acknowledgment can go a long way in building morale and fostering cohesion among teams.

These same principles also apply to virtual communication platforms like video chat or emails. Women should pay attention to how they present themselves in these spaces, as the same body language cues can still be detected. While it is harder to read reactions over virtual platforms, being aware of one's non-verbal communication can help make sure that their message is heard and understood. Understanding how to properly use body language can give women the confidence they need to command respect and create meaningful connections. It is a key tool for women to effectively communicate their ideas and stand out in the workplace. With practice, mastering these skills can help women gain an edge in their professional lives.

By taking the time to understand body language, women can make sure that their message is communicated loud and clear. It opens up a world of opportunities for them to be taken seriously, demonstrate confidence, and get ahead in their careers. With the right attitude and knowledge of body language cues, women are well-equipped to succeed in the workplace.

Giving feedback is a key part of professional development - it can help people learn, grow, and improve. However, delivering constructive criticism in the workplace isn't always easy. Women should be aware that body language plays an important role when it comes to providing feedback.

For instance, making eye contact and maintaining an open posture are important indicators of respect and trust. Additionally, using positive body language language when giving critiques can help to create a productive atmosphere where people feel safe expressing themselves and learning from their mistakes.

Overall, body language is an invaluable tool for women in the workplace. It can be used to communicate their ideas clearly, gain respect, and demonstrate leadership. By understanding the power of body language, women are well-positioned to succeed in their professional lives.

By mastering body language, women can effectively express themselves in the workplace - creating an environment where their ideas and opinions are valued. Through careful observation and practice, they will be able to establish trust with their colleagues, build strong relationships, and contribute to a more harmonious work culture.

Finally, one should also be aware that body language is a two-way street - focusing on both sending and receiving cues can help create meaningful connections and foster better communication between colleagues. Taking the time to observe how others use body language can help to better one's own understanding of nonverbal communication. With this knowledge, women can further enhance their professional relationships and make a lasting impact in the workplace.

Chapter 3.3 Expressing Yourself with Empathy

Empathy serves as a powerful tool in a woman's arsenal, allowing for profound connections with others. It is the ability to understand and share the feelings of those around us, creating a sense of shared experiences and mutual understanding. This empathetic approach extends beyond personal relationships, permeating professional environments, social situations, and even global issues. It is through empathy that women can express themselves authentically, fostering more meaningful relationships and promoting an atmosphere of mutual respect and understanding.

Empathy also has the power to bridge divides, build bridges between cultures and ideologies, and create a more inclusive society. By putting ourselves in another's shoes, we can gain a greater understanding of their perspective. We can come to appreciate the unique experiences each individual brings and adapt our approach accordingly. In doing so, we not only create an environment that is more conducive to collaboration, but we also learn and grow from experiencing the perspectives of others. Furthermore, empathy can lead to positive change on a much larger scale as it allows us to identify with injustices and strive for equality.

In order to cultivate greater empathy in our lives, it is important to practice active listening and pay close attention to body language and verbal cues. By taking the time to really listen, we can better understand the emotions and experiences of those around us. We can also focus on building positive relationships by displaying kindness and compassion towards others. Finally, it is essential that we take a moment to pause and reflect on our own biases and conscious choices in order to ensure that we are exhibiting empathy in a genuine manner.

By taking the time to understand, empathize, and bridge divides we can create a more inclusive and equitable society for all. Through empathy, we all have the power to make a difference in our lives and the world around us. Together, we can create a better future.

By looking to the future and actively engaging in conversations that center around empathy, understanding, and inclusivity, we can begin to break down barriers that exist between us. We can learn from each other's experiences and come together to create meaningful dialogue about how we can work together to make our world a more equitable place. With a focus on empathy, we can create a better future for generations to come. Through education and understanding, we can move forward as one and create an environment of respect and acceptance for all. Together, we have the power to make meaningful change happen. Let us commit to actively engaging in conversations around empathy and strive for a better tomorrow. The future is calling us to act. Let's answer.

By cultivating empathy, we can learn to appreciate and value the perspectives of others, regardless of their background or circumstances. We can work together to foster understanding and acceptance for all people through listening, dialogue, and collaboration. With a shared commitment to empathy, we can bridge divides that exist between us and create a more equitable society. It is our responsibility to reframe the conversations we have with one another in order to create meaningful change. We must also refe hand, by utilizing technology, we can reach further than ever before while still maintaining our core values of empathy and respect for each other. Together, let us strive for a world of equity and understanding.

It is up to each of us to commit to the cause of empathy and strive for a better future. We can all take responsibility by engaging in conversations that center around understanding, acceptance, and collaboration. Let us come together and work towards creating a more equitable world for all. By actively listening to the perspectives of others, we can foster meaningful dialogue and create an environment of acceptance and respect. With open hearts and minds, we can create a bright future for all. Let us rise to the challenge and join together in our mission to cultivate empathy for generations to come.

We are the ones that can bring about meaningful change. Let us answer the call and move forward as one towards a brighter tomorrow. Together, let us create a world of understanding, appreciation, and acceptance for all. Let us work together to bridge divide that exists between us and build a better future for everyone. We can do this by cultivating empathy in our communities and actively listening to the perspectives of others. With open hearts and minds, let us come together and use our collective power to create a more equitable society for all. Together, we can make a lasting impact on the world. Let us take up this challenge and move forward with courage and resilience.

Chapter 4 Understanding Her Needs

The key to understanding a woman's needs is communication, empathy, and respect. Women, like all individuals, have a unique blend of emotional, intellectual, and physical needs that contribute to their overall well-being.

Emotional needs often involve feeling loved, appreciated, and secure. This can be demonstrated through words of affirmation, quality time, thoughtful gestures, and acts of kindness. Remember, showing empathy during challenging times can also make a significant difference. Intellectual needs may include engaging in stimulating conversations, being encouraged to pursue personal passions or career aspirations, and having their ideas and opinions valued.

Physical needs vary greatly among individuals but may encompass maintaining physical health, appreciating personal space, or understanding intimate needs. Also, one of the important needs is the necessity for independence. Women need to feel that they are capable, autonomous individuals who can make their own decisions, whether about their careers, their bodies, or their lives in general.

In conclusion, understanding a woman's needs is not a one-size-fits-all scenario. It requires genuine effort, patience, and open-mindedness to comprehend and respect the needs of every unique individual. Remember, the foundation of understanding any person's needs, regardless of gender, lies in open communication, mutual respect, and empathy.

Likewise, it is important to remain aware of the evolution of a woman's needs as her life circumstances change and provide support accordingly. Asking open-ended questions about what she wants or needs in certain situations can be a great way to stay connected and build trust. By approaching every relationship with these attitudes and practices, mutual understanding and respect will blossom.

Creating an environment of acceptance and understanding is also essential to meeting a woman's needs. This means respecting her personal boundaries, avoiding judgment and criticism, allowing her to make mistakes without ridicule, and validating her feelings. A safe emotional space is the cornerstone of any meaningful relationship. By keeping these elements in mind, it will be easier to foster healthy relationships with those we care about.

Additionally, being aware of the social and cultural context in which a woman exists is essential. This means understanding the implicit biases that are embedded within society, such as racism, sexism, ableism, or other forms of oppression. When we recognize and honor these inherent differences in experience and perspective, it can go a long way towards creating an atmosphere of inclusion and acceptance.

Recognizing and appreciating the varied needs of women can be a challenge in our fast-paced world. But by taking the time to listen, learn, and cultivate understanding, meaningful relationships can be nurtured and strengthened for all involved. Embracing this mindful approach to communication is key to ensuring that every woman's needs are met with respect and acceptance.

By being mindful of these elements, it will be easier to create an atmosphere of understanding and respect in any relationship. Whether with family members, friends, or romantic partners, investing time into building a trusting and safe emotional space will only serve to benefit both sides. With a little effort, we can create an environment that is inclusive and empowering for women everywhere.

At the same time, it is important to remember that relationships take two parties to be successful. Women need to demand respect by setting boundaries when necessary and advocating for their own needs. It is only through mutual understanding and an appreciation of each other's unique perspectives that meaningful relationships are created and sustained. By fostering a sense of mutual understanding, we can build an environment of acceptance and respect that will benefit all parties involved.

Finally, it is important to recognize that relationships are a two-way street and mutual respect must be present for any relationship to grow and thrive. Women should be encouraged to voice their needs and opinions in order for these needs to be heard and met. Allowing both parties equal opportunities to express themselves is a crucial step in creating meaningful connections with those around us. In doing so, we can create an environment of trust and understanding that will foster connection with others and support the growth of both parties in any relationship.

Chapter 4.1 Physical Needs and Intimacy

A woman's physical needs and intimacy are crucial aspects of her overall well-being. They encompass a spectrum of needs like a balanced diet, regular exercise, adequate sleep, and proper healthcare. Intimacy, on the other hand, is more than just physical closeness. It includes emotional closeness, trust, understanding, affection, and open communication. Fulfilling these needs can significantly enhance a woman's health, self-esteem, and relationships, contributing to her overall quality of life.

It is important for women to recognize their own physical and emotional needs, as well as those of the people in their lives. Taking time to nurture relationships and create intimate moments with loved ones can help foster understanding and trust. Allocating a regular time for self-care activities such as yoga, relaxation, journaling or meditation can also help promote a healthy balance between physical and emotional needs. Additionally, seeking help from mental health professionals or talking to friends and family can be beneficial in developing strategies to meet both physical and emotional needs. Doing so can improve a woman's overall sense of well-being.

It is also important for women to practice self-love and appreciation, as this can lead to improved self-esteem and confidence. Practicing self-care, setting personal boundaries and expressing feelings openly are all important ways to boost self-worth. When a woman is aware of her physical and emotional needs and works to prioritize them in her life, she can lead a more fulfilling and purposeful life.

It is essential for women to take an active role in taking care of their physical and emotional needs. Engaging in activities that promote wellness, such as exercise, proper nutrition, adequate sleep, and self-care can help women feel more connected to themselves and others. Recognizing the importance of developing intimate relationships with loved ones can also lead to improved overall health and well-being. By prioritizing their physical and emotional needs, women can create a balanced and fulfilling life.

Making time for meaningful conversations with friends, family or colleagues can be a great way to nurture relationships and feel connected. Having an open conversation about feelings can help build trust and understanding, as well as promote peace of mind. Additionally, maintaining healthy habits such as eating nutritious foods and getting enough sleep helps keep the body and mind energized. Taking part in enjoyable activities can also help to reduce stress and boost mood.

In addition, setting realistic goals and engaging in positive self-talk can help women feel more empowered and accomplished. These tools can be used as a means of achieving personal growth, reaching potential goals, and building self-esteem. The importance of having a strong support system cannot be understated; connecting with friends and family, or even joining a group or organization can help give women the support they need to keep striving towards their goals.

It is essential for women to focus on self-love and appreciation. Taking part in activities that help increase self-awareness can be beneficial in helping to identify areas of growth and development. It is important to be mindful of how to nurture individual strengths and talents, as these are often vital ingredients for a fulfilled life. Taking care of oneself and allowing time for self-reflection can help nurture a positive outlook and increase overall happiness.

Women have an incredible ability to lead inspiring lives when provided with the right resources. By taking steps towards self-care, women can create positive experiences that help foster healthy mindsets and enrich their lives. Empowerment can be found in a variety of forms, but it is ultimately up to the individual to make the most of every opportunity. Through self-care and personal growth, women can discover inner strength and resilience while paving the way for healthier futures.

By creating a personalized self-care routine, women can make positive changes that help improve their mental health and overall wellbeing. Establishing a healthy balance between work and leisure activities is key to achieving personal goals and feeling fulfilled. Engaging in regular exercise, such as yoga or running, can be helpful in reducing stress levels and improving mood. In addition, finding time for hobbies or creative activities can provide an outlet for creative expression and help create a sense of purpose.

It is important for women to take the time to appreciate their accomplishments and recognize the progress they have made in life. Celebrating successes, big or small, can help boost self-confidence and provide motivation to keep striving towards personal goals. Similarly, taking breaks from work or life in general can be beneficial for achieving clarity and perspective. Whether it is a short walk in nature, a trip to the beach or an indulgent spa day with friends, taking time out to relax and recharge can remove any feelings of stress and anxiety.

By practicing self-care, women can become better equipped to tackle life's challenges and build healthier lives. Ultimately, self-care is about taking the time to look after one's own needs and engage in activities that bring joy and fulfillment. While it may take time and effort to establish a personal routine, it is well worth the effort for the long-term benefits that self-care provides. With a solid foundation of self-care, women can unlock their true potential and create the life they desire.

Finally, it is important to remember that self-care comes in many forms and that every woman's needs are different. It is essential to invest time in creating a routine that works for each individual, as this can provide an effective way to manage stress and build resilience. Taking the time to focus on one's physical, mental, and emotional needs is essential in feeling content with life. It is by committing to self-care that women can take control of their lives and create a more fulfilling future.

Chapter 4.2 Emotional Support and Validation

Women, like all individuals, require emotional support and validation. Recognizing their feelings, experiences, and accomplishments can be profoundly impactful, fostering a sense of worth and boosting self-esteem. "We understand and acknowledge your experiences and feelings. Your strength, resilience, and unique perspective are truly inspiring. Your journey, with all its trials and triumphs, is valid and important. Never doubt your value and remember that your emotions are a significant part of who you are, deserving respect and understanding."

By validating women's experiences, feelings, and perspectives, we can help shape healthier relationships with the world around them. We must ensure that our language reflects respect for women in all of its facets: verbal, written, physical and social. This includes listening without judgement and speaking to women with kindness and acceptance. By creating an inclusive environment where everyone is valued equally, we can create a more just world with greater understanding and empathy for all.

We must also strive to ensure that women are given the same opportunities as men, particularly in fields where they have traditionally been underrepresented. We must encourage initiatives which provide mentorship, leadership training, and access to resources in order to broaden the range of possibilities available for women. By investing in their potential, we can create a society that celebrates the unique talents of each individual.

Together, let us continue to work towards creating a more just future for all women. By recognizing the value of each individual's unique perspectives, we can foster an environment which celebrates diversity and encourages collaboration instead of competition. Let us strive to promote a culture of respect and inclusivity, one which recognizes the importance of all voices and provides equal opportunities for everyone. In doing so, we can create a brighter future for us all.

Let us continue to move forward with an open mind and heart, embracing diversity and striving to create an equitable society where every woman is respected and valued. With each step we take towards equality, we can make a difference in the lives of women around the world. Together, let us create a future that celebrates and honors the contributions of all.

Thank you for your commitment to building an equal and just society. Every effort counts and together we can create lasting change in empowering women everywhere. Let us continue to work hand-in-hand towards a brighter future for all.

Let us make sure to take time to recognize and celebrate the important work being done by individuals who are speaking out against discrimination, violence, and inequality. Let us also remember those individuals who have worked tirelessly to advance the cause of women's rights throughout history. It is through their legacy that we can build a better world for all of us.

Let us remember that progress towards a more equitable society is in our hands. We can create lasting change by standing together and speaking out against injustice and inequality, while also creating meaningful opportunities for women to reach their full potential. With courage, resilience, and determination, we can create a better world where all women are empowered to achieve their dreams.

Together, let us join forces to create a world built on respect, understanding and acceptance for all women. Let us continue the fight for gender equality and human rights for everyone around the globe. Our commitment to justice and fairness will bring about an era of hope and opportunity for generations to come. Let us be part of a better future for all women.

Let us take the time to learn from each other, share our stories and experiences, and ensure that everyone has equal access to resources. By working together and investing in women's education, health care, economic security, and political participation, we can create a world where all women have the opportunity to thrive. This future is within our reach—let us work together to make it a reality.

Let us also work to create an environment in which all women feel safe and secure, free from violence and discrimination. Let us ensure that our laws protect the rights of women so that they can fully participate in society without fear or retribution. By standing together and advocating for gender equality, we can build a world where everyone is valued and respected.

Finally, we must strive to create an environment which is free from discrimination and violence. We must speak out against harassment in all its forms and ensure that women are safe and respected in all aspects of their lives. Through our commitment to equality, justice, and respect for all, we can create a world where women feel empowered to pursue their passions and contribute to meaningful progress in society.

Chapter 4.3 Intellectual Stimulation

Intellectual stimulation is a vital aspect of personal growth and development for every individual, including women. Engaging in intellectually stimulating activities such as reading, solving puzzles, or learning new skills can greatly enhance cognitive abilities, foster creativity, and boost self-confidence. It paves the way for women to broaden their horizons, encouraging critical and innovative thinking. This intellectual pursuit not only enriches personal life but also contributes positively to professional advancement, empowering women to achieve their goals in an increasingly knowledge-driven society.

Moreover, intellectual stimulation is a great way for women to stay connected with their peers and the larger community. By engaging in meaningful conversations, being open to diverse perspectives, and expanding one's knowledge of current events and topics, women can become more aware of the world around them. Such engagement not only helps strengthen existing relationships but also fosters new ones. It allows women to build their social circles, share ideas, and learn from the experiences of others. Ultimately, intellectual stimulation provides women with an opportunity to grow personally and professionally while remaining connected with the larger community.

Intellectual stimulation can also be a way for women to find purpose in life. By engaging in meaningful activities that require creative and critical thinking skills, women can discover their passions and find fulfillment in life. With the right set of skills, they can translate this newfound purpose into tangible actions that positively impact society. Whether it's by writing a book, teaching others, or taking on an innovative project, intellectual stimulation helps women unlock their full potential and make meaningful contributions to the world.

In a nutshell, engaging in intellectually stimulating activities is a great way for women to stay connected with the world, foster meaningful relationships, and find purpose in life. By pursuing knowledge and creativity, women can achieve personal growth while making lasting contributions to society. In short, intellectual stimulation empowers women to reach their full potential!

Furthermore, engaging in intellectually stimulating activities can also be an important tool in managing stress and anxiety. When faced with challenging moments, turning to intellectually stimulating activities can provide a much-needed distraction from the chaos of daily life. It gives women an opportunity to step back and clear their minds while stirring up creativity and innovation. In this way, women can develop effective coping mechanisms for dealing with their anxieties in healthy ways.

Finally, intellectual stimulation also provides a chance for women to stay connected with each other and build support systems. By engaging in stimulating activities like book clubs, seminars, or lectures, women can find common ground and form meaningful connections with others. This helps create an empowering environment where the exchange of ideas is valued and celebrated.

Chapter 5 Love Languages and Appreciation

Love languages and appreciation are essential aspects of any relationship, including the appreciation of a woman. The concept of "love languages" was popularized by Dr. Gary Chapman in his book "The 5 Love Languages." According to this theory, people have different ways of giving and receiving love, and understanding each other's love language can significantly improve the emotional connection and satisfaction within a relationship.

The five love languages are:

- Words of Affirmation: This love language involves expressing love and appreciation through verbal compliments, kind words, and encouragement. For a woman whose primary love language is words of affirmation, heartfelt praise and positive affirmations can make her feel deeply loved and cherished.

- Acts of Service: This love language revolves around doing things for your partner that will make their life easier and more comfortable. For a woman who appreciates acts of service, taking care of tasks or responsibilities, and offering help or support can be highly meaningful and demonstrate your love for her.

- Receiving Gifts: Some people feel most loved when they receive thoughtful gifts. It's not about materialism but rather the sentiment and effort put into choosing the right gift. For a woman with this love language, giving her thoughtful presents can speak volumes about your affection.

- Quality Time: Quality time is about giving someone your undivided attention and engaging in meaningful activities together. For a woman whose primary love language is quality time, spending quality moments together and showing genuine interest in her life and thoughts is vital.
- Physical Touch: Physical touch includes non-sexual affection such as hugging, holding hands, cuddling, and gentle touches. For a woman whose love language is physical touch, physical intimacy and affection are essential expressions of love and appreciation.

It's important to note that everyone is unique, and individuals may have different combinations or degrees of these love languages. To understand and appreciate a woman better, open communication is key. You can ask her directly or observe her reactions and responses to different gestures to identify her love language.

Lastly, remember that showing appreciation and love should be a genuine expression of your feelings and not just a checklist of tasks. When you authentically appreciate and love a woman based on her preferences and needs, it fosters a deeper and more meaningful connection in the relationship.

Chapter 5.1 The Five Love Languages

In the world of relationships, there exists a profound secret to unlocking lasting love and creating an unbreakable emotional connection with your partner. This secret lies in understanding and speaking the language of love, a language that transcends words and actions, yet resonates deeply within the core of every individual. Dr. Gary Chapman, a renowned marriage counselor and author, discovered this language and unveiled its mysteries to the world through his groundbreaking concept known as "The Five Love Languages."

The Language of Words: Affirmation and Encouragement

As we delve into the first love language, we find ourselves immersed in the beauty of words. For some, words possess a unique power to affirm, uplift, and inspire. A kind compliment, a heartfelt "I love you," or a simple "You are appreciated" can fill the heart of these individuals with boundless joy and reassurance. The language of words transcends the mundane and transforms relationships into a sanctuary of love and support.

THE LANGUAGE OF ACTIONS: Love in Motion

Step into the realm of actions, where love finds its expression through deeds rather than words. Acts of service become the profound currency of affection for those whose love language lies here. The power of love is seen in the willingness to lend a helping hand, to shoulder burdens, and to embrace responsibilities together. Whether it's doing the dishes, walking the dog, or surprising your partner with their favorite meal after a long day, these gestures of love create an unbreakable bond of care and devotion.

The Language of Gifts: Symbols of Love

In this chapter, we explore how love can be wrapped in paper and tied with ribbons. For some, the language of gifts carries immense significance. It is not the price tag that matters but the thought and effort behind the gesture. A carefully chosen present can speak volumes about love, appreciation, and the deep connection between two souls. These tangible symbols of love become cherished mementos, reminding individuals of the affection they share and the importance of their bond.

The Language of Quality Time: Presence and Intimacy

As we turn the pages to the language of quality time, we encounter the profound essence of presence. In today's fast-paced world, time has become a precious commodity. To those who speak this love language, undivided attention and meaningful moments are the building blocks of a strong relationship. It is not merely about being in the same room but engaging with each other, sharing experiences, and creating memories that will last a lifetime. Quality time is an investment in love's eternal dividends.

The Language of Touch: The Power of Connection

Finally, we arrive at the language of touch, where love is felt through physical expressions of affection. A gentle touch, a warm embrace, or a soft caress can convey a depth of emotion that words alone cannot capture. Physical touch is a language that speaks to the primal nature of human beings—the need for comfort, security, and the knowledge that one is cherished beyond words.

Fluency in Love: Embracing Diversity

Every person's love language is unique, like a fingerprint that distinguishes them from the rest. In the journey of love, understanding and fluently speaking each other's love languages become the keys to a fulfilling and lasting relationship. By knowing your partner's love language, you become empowered to nurture and strengthen your bond in ways that resonate deeply with them. Simultaneously, communicating your love language allows your partner to express affection in a language that fills your heart to the brim.

As we conclude this chapter on the Five Love Languages, let us remember that love is a tapestry woven from different threads, each one adding its beauty to the whole. By embracing and celebrating the diversity of love languages, we can create relationships that are boundless in their depth, timeless in their endurance, and radiant in their love. So, dear reader, I invite you to explore the love languages with an open heart, and may you uncover the secrets that will forever enrich your journey of love and connection.

Chapter 5.2 Discovering Her Love Language

Discovering your partner's love language requires attentive observation, open communication, and a willingness to make an effort to understand their preferences. Here are some steps to help you discover her love language:

- Pay attention to her actions and expressions: Observe how she expresses love and affection towards others, including friends, family, and pets. Does she frequently offer words of affirmation, give thoughtful gifts, prioritize spending quality time, engage in acts of service, or initiate physical touch? Notice any patterns in her behavior.
- Listen to her hints and comments: Sometimes, people drop subtle hints or make comments about what they appreciate or wish for in a relationship. Pay attention to any statements she makes about love, affection, or what she values in a partner.
- Reflect on her complaints or frustrations: Take note of any complaints or frustrations she may have expressed in the past. For example, if she mentions feeling neglected when you haven't spent quality time together, it could be an indication that quality time is her love language.
- Observe her response to your actions: When you express love or affection in different ways, take note of her reactions. Does she seem particularly delighted when you give her a thoughtful gift, or does she light up when you compliment

her?

- Communicate openly: Initiate a conversation about love languages and express your interest in understanding how she feels most loved and appreciated. You can mention that you came across the concept of love languages and would like to learn more about what makes her feel loved.
- Ask her directly: Sometimes, direct communication is the best approach. Ask her how she prefers to receive love and affection. You can share the concept of the five love languages and inquire which one(s) resonate most with her.
- Experiment and adapt: Be willing to try different approaches based on your observations and conversations. Put effort into expressing love in ways that align with her love language and observe how she responds.
- Be patient and understanding: Discovering someone's love language may take time, so be patient and understanding throughout the process. Remember that everyone is unique, and her love language might be a combination of different elements.

By taking the time to observe, listen, and communicate openly with your partner, you can better understand her love language and strengthen your connection by expressing love in ways that truly resonate with her. Keep in mind that learning each other's love languages is an ongoing process, and it can lead to a more fulfilling and harmonious relationship.

Chapter 5.3 Showing Appreciation and Affection

Appreciation and affection are two distinct but interconnected emotions that play essential roles in human relationships and well-being. Let's explore each of these emotions separately:

- Appreciation: Appreciation refers to the recognition and gratitude we feel towards someone or something for their positive qualities, actions, or contributions. It involves acknowledging and valuing the efforts, kindness, support, or achievements of others. When we appreciate someone, we focus on the positive aspects of their character and actions, which can enhance our connection with them and create a positive atmosphere in relationships.

Appreciation can be expressed in various ways, such as through words of thanks, compliments, praise, or gestures of recognition. It strengthens bonds and fosters a sense of being valued and respected. In personal relationships, expressing appreciation can make people feel loved and cherished, leading to increased emotional intimacy.

- Affection: Affection is a warm and tender feeling we have for others, typically arising from a sense of care, fondness, or attachment. It involves emotions such as love, tenderness, warmth, and compassion. Affectionate behavior can include physical touch, comforting words, acts of kindness, and gestures that demonstrate care and concern.

Affection is a fundamental human need, and it's essential for building healthy relationships. It can exist in various forms, from platonic friendships to romantic partnerships and family connections. Displaying affection fosters emotional closeness, boosts trust, and creates a sense of emotional security, which is vital for overall well-being.

The Connection Between Appreciation and Affection: Appreciation and affection are often intertwined. When we feel affectionate towards someone, we are more inclined to appreciate them and vice versa. Showing appreciation is an act of affection, and affectionate gestures often come from a place of appreciation.

In relationships, expressing appreciation can reinforce the bond of affection. For example, expressing gratitude and showing affection to a romantic partner can deepen the emotional connection and strengthen the love between them. Similarly, in friendships, expressing appreciation for a friend's support or kindness can enhance the affectionate bond between friends.

In summary, appreciation and affection are powerful emotions that contribute to the positive dynamics of relationships. Expressing gratitude and showing affection towards others are essential components of building and maintaining meaningful and fulfilling connections with the people in our lives. These emotions promote empathy, kindness, and emotional intimacy, fostering a sense of belonging and happiness in both personal and social settings.

Chapter 6 Managing Conflicts and Disagreements

Conflict is an inevitable part of human interactions, and disagreements can arise in various settings, including professional environments, personal relationships, and social interactions. It is essential to handle conflicts and disagreements with sensitivity and respect, especially when dealing with women. In this essay, we will explore strategies for effectively managing conflicts and disagreements with women, emphasizing the importance of empathy, active listening, and mutual understanding.

Understanding the Gender Perspective

To navigate conflicts and disagreements with women effectively, it is crucial to recognize the unique challenges they might face. Women often experience societal expectations and gender-related biases that can influence their behavior, decision-making, and communication style. To foster a positive resolution, it is essential to approach conflicts with an open mind and without preconceived notions.

Empathy as a Key Component

Empathy is the ability to understand and share the feelings of others genuinely. It plays a vital role in managing conflicts and disagreements with women. When engaging in discussions with women, taking the time to empathize with their emotions and experiences can help in building trust and rapport.

By empathizing, we validate their feelings and perspectives, creating a safe environment for open communication. This acknowledgment helps women feel heard and respected, leading to a more productive resolution of conflicts.

Active Listening for Effective Communication

Active listening is another critical skill in resolving conflicts with women. It involves giving undivided attention to the speaker, being fully present, and seeking to comprehend the underlying concerns. During disagreements, women may face challenges in expressing themselves due to social or cultural norms. Active listening allows them to communicate freely and ensures that their voices are heard and acknowledged.

Resist the temptation to interrupt or dominate the conversation, as this can lead to further frustration and escalate the conflict. Instead, focus on understanding their viewpoints and reflecting back on what they've expressed to confirm that you comprehend their position accurately.

Promoting Inclusivity and Equality

A productive approach to managing conflicts with women involves fostering an inclusive and equal environment. Be mindful of unintentional biases and ensure that women have equal opportunities to voice their opinions and contribute to discussions. Encourage an atmosphere where diverse perspectives are valued and respected.

Avoiding Gender Stereotypes

During disagreements, it is essential to steer clear of gender stereotypes that may perpetuate inequality or dismiss women's concerns. Avoid making assumptions based on gender and instead focus on the specific issues at hand. By treating women as individuals with unique thoughts and opinions, you demonstrate respect and create an environment conducive to constructive dialogue.

Seeking Win-Win Solutions

The goal of managing conflicts and disagreements should always be to find win-win solutions where all parties feel satisfied with the outcome. Collaborative problem-solving allows for a fair and balanced resolution, taking into account the needs and perspectives of all involved, including women.

When negotiating, be open to compromise and find common ground to bridge the gap. Avoid pushing for a one-sided resolution that may disregard the concerns of women. Strive for a solution that acknowledges and respects the interests of everyone involved.

Conclusion

Managing conflicts and disagreements with women requires a thoughtful and empathetic approach. By understanding the unique challenges they may face and actively listening to their perspectives, we create an atmosphere where productive discussions can occur. Empathy and inclusivity are key components in fostering mutual understanding and finding win-win solutions to conflicts. Let us all strive to create a world where women's voices are heard and respected, and conflicts are resolved with understanding and empathy. Through such efforts, we can build stronger relationships and a more harmonious society for everyone.

Chapter 6.1 Common Relationship Challenges

Conflict is an inevitable part of human interactions, and disagreements can arise in various settings, including professional environments, personal relationships, and social interactions. It is essential to handle conflicts and disagreements with sensitivity and respect, especially when dealing with women. In this essay, we will explore strategies for effectively managing conflicts and disagreements with women, emphasizing the importance of empathy, active listening, and mutual understanding.

To navigate conflicts and disagreements with women effectively, it is crucial to recognize the unique challenges they might face. Women often experience societal expectations and gender-related biases that can influence their behavior, decision-making, and communication style. To foster a positive resolution, it is essential to approach conflicts with an open mind and without preconceived notions.

Empathy is the ability to understand and share the feelings of others genuinely. It plays a vital role in managing conflicts and disagreements with women. When engaging in discussions with women, taking the time to empathize with their emotions and experiences can help in building trust and rapport.

By empathizing, we validate their feelings and perspectives, creating a safe environment for open communication. This acknowledgment helps women feel heard and respected, leading to a more productive resolution of conflicts.

Active Listening for Effective Communication

Active listening is another critical skill in resolving conflicts with women. It involves giving undivided attention to the speaker, being fully present, and seeking to comprehend the underlying concerns. During disagreements, women may face challenges in expressing themselves due to social or cultural norms. Active listening allows them to communicate freely and ensures that their voices are heard and acknowledged. Resist the temptation to interrupt or dominate the conversation, as this can lead to further frustration and escalate the conflict. Instead, focus on understanding

A productive approach to managing conflicts with women involves fostering an inclusive and equal environment. Be mindful of unintentional biases and ensure that women have equal opportunities to voice their opinions and contribute to discussions. Encourage an atmosphere where diverse perspectives are valued and respected.

During disagreements, it is essential to steer clear of gender stereotypes that may perpetuate inequality or dismiss women's concerns. Avoid making assumptions based on gender and instead focus on the specific issues at hand. By treating women as individuals with unique thoughts and opinions, you demonstrate respect and create an environment conducive to constructive dialogue.

The goal of managing conflicts and disagreements should always be to find win-win solutions where all parties feel satisfied with the outcome. Collaborative problem-solving allows for a fair and balanced resolution, taking into account the needs and perspectives of all involved, including women.

When negotiating, be open to compromise and find common ground to bridge the gap. Avoid pushing for a one-sided resolution that may disregard the concerns of women. Strive for a solution that acknowledges and respects the interests of everyone involved.

Conclusion

Managing conflicts and disagreements with women requires a thoughtful and empathetic approach. By understanding the unique challenges they may face and actively listening to their perspectives, we create an atmosphere where productive discussions can occur. Empathy and inclusivity are key components in fostering mutual understanding and finding win-win solutions to conflicts. Let us all strive to create a world where women's voices are heard and respected, and conflicts are resolved with understanding and empathy. Through such efforts, we can build stronger relationships and a more harmonious society for everyone.

Chapter 6.2 Conflict Resolution Strategies

Conflict is an inevitable part of human interactions, and it is essential to address it with care and sensitivity. When it comes to resolving conflicts with women, understanding their unique perspectives and experiences is crucial for successful resolution. In this essay, we will explore conflict resolution strategies that focus on empathy, active listening, and collaboration to foster understanding and build stronger relationships with women.

- Emphasizing Empathy

One of the fundamental aspects of conflict resolution with women is demonstrating empathy. Women, like anyone else, want their feelings and experiences to be understood and acknowledged. Showing empathy involves putting oneself in the other person's shoes and genuinely trying to comprehend their emotions. This may require suspending judgment and preconceived notions to better understand the individual's perspective.

- Active Listening

Active listening plays a pivotal role in resolving conflicts with women. Listening attentively, without interruption or judgment, allows women to express themselves fully. Active listening involves maintaining eye contact, nodding to show understanding, and using verbal cues to convey engagement. When women feel heard and respected, they are more likely to reciprocate and participate constructively in finding solutions.

- Avoiding Gender Stereotypes

It is crucial to be conscious of gender stereotypes that can affect conflict resolution. Women have often faced societal expectations that might influence how they express themselves during conflicts. As conflict resolution partners, we must avoid assumptions based on these stereotypes and instead focus on the individual's unique needs and perspectives.

- Collaboration over Competition

A collaborative approach to conflict resolution fosters a sense of partnership and equality. Rather than engaging in a competitive mindset, work together as a team to find mutually beneficial solutions. Encouraging open dialogue, brainstorming, and valuing diverse opinions can lead to innovative resolutions that benefit all parties involved.

- Respecting Personal Boundaries

During the conflict resolution process, respecting personal boundaries is essential. Women, like anyone else, may need time and space to process their emotions before discussing the conflict further. Pressuring them to engage before they are ready can lead to heightened tensions and hinder resolution efforts. Patience and understanding go a long way in creating a safe and supportive environment for conflict resolution.

- Communicating with "I" Statements

Using "I" statements during discussions allows individuals to express their emotions and concerns without sounding accusatory. For instance, saying "I feel hurt when..." instead of "You always..." creates a more conducive atmosphere for open communication. This approach prevents defensiveness and fosters empathy, paving the way for a more constructive conversation.

- Acknowledging Strengths and Contributions

Recognizing and appreciating the strengths and contributions of women during conflict resolution can strengthen relationships. Acknowledging their valuable insights and unique abilities fosters a sense of inclusion and empowerment, leading to increased cooperation in finding solutions.

Conclusion

Conflict resolution with women requires sensitivity, empathy, and an open-minded approach. By actively listening, avoiding gender stereotypes, and fostering collaboration, conflicts can be transformed into opportunities for growth and understanding. Building stronger relationships with women through effective conflict resolution will not only lead to healthier interactions but also promote gender equality and mutual respect in all aspects of life.

Chapter 6.3 Fighting Fairly and Constructively

Finding a way to resolve conflicts and disputes in a relationship can be difficult. When couples get into heated disagreements, it's natural to want to state our point quickly and fiercely, with no room for negotiation or compromise. But this approach isn't healthy for any relationship. Being able to fight fairly and constructively is key to moving forward instead of going in circles.

The first step is to recognize that the conflict isn't about winning or being right, but rather finding a resolution that works for both people. This means approaching issues with open-mindedness and understanding. It may be helpful to take a break from the discussion if things start getting heated and come back when you can both approach it with cooler heads.

It's also important to stay on the same page and focus on the issue at hand. You and your partner should take turns expressing yourselves, listening to each other without interruption, and trying to find a mutually agreeable solution. This means being honest about how you feel and avoiding blaming or shaming language.

We all want our relationships to be healthy and happy, which is why it's important to learn how to fight fairly and constructively. Not only will this help you work through conflicts more easily, but it will also strengthen your bond in the long run.

It can take some practice to get used to constructive conflict resolution. But if both people are committed to finding a peaceful resolution that works for both of you, it's possible to come out of a disagreement with better understanding and clarity. Being able to talk openly about difficult topics is an essential part of any healthy relationship.

When conflicts arise, it's important to take the time to find a constructive resolution that works for everyone involved. This doesn't mean avoiding difficult conversations; rather, it means learning to approach them with understanding and open-mindedness. Through constructive conflict resolution, you can learn how to express yourself honestly while still finding a peaceful solution that works for everyone involved. By learning these skills, you'll be able to build trust and strengthen your relationship in the long run.

Remember, it's okay to disagree as long as both parties are willing to learn from each other and move forward together. Constructive conflict resolution is key to any healthy relationship, so don't be afraid to practice it!

Of course, not all disagreements can be solved through constructive conflict resolution alone. If you find yourself in a situation that feels too intense or difficult to resolve on your own, it's important to reach out for help. Seeking professional guidance can provide you with tools and strategies to tackle difficult conversations in a productive way.

Constructive conflict resolution doesn't have to be intimidating or scary. By learning how to effectively communicate with each other, you can find solutions that work for both of you and create a stronger bond as a result. Keep an open mind and stay focused on finding a positive outcome - you'll be surprised by how much progress can be made in even the most difficult conversations!

At the end of the day, it's important to remember that disagreements are a normal part of life. With a little bit of patience and understanding, you'll be able to find common ground and better understand each other's perspectives. Constructive conflict resolution can be a powerful tool for any relationship - use it to your advantage!

If you're feeling overwhelmed by a situation, take a break and come back to it with a fresh perspective. Re-frame your conversation in terms of what each person is trying to achieve and come up with realistic goals that everyone can agree on. This will help both parties move closer towards understanding one another and finding a resolution that works for both sides.

It's also important to remember that constructive conflict resolution is not always about finding a "right" or "wrong" answer. Many times, it's simply about discovering common ground and different perspectives. So take your time, be patient with each other, and create an opportunity for productive dialogue - you'll be surprised at how much progress can be made when you work together!

Finally, don't forget to take some time for yourself. Conflict can be exhausting, both mentally and physically. Give yourself a break every now and then - take a walk, listen to music, or just sit in silence for a while - whatever helps you relax and regain your composure. Taking care of yourself is an important part of the process, and will help you be better prepared to handle any disagreements that may arise.

Chapter 7 Emotional Well-Being and Mental Health

Emotional well-being and mental health are crucial aspects of a woman's overall health. These encompass a woman's ability to manage stress, maintain positive relationships, and handle the ups and downs of daily life. Women often face unique mental health challenges, such as hormonal fluctuations related to menstruation, pregnancy, or menopause, that can have a significant impact on their emotional well-being. Recognizing these factors and promoting open dialogues about mental health can help in fostering a culture of understanding and support, thus leading to improved mental health outcomes for women.

It is important that women understand the signs and symptoms of mental health conditions in order to seek help when needed. Common mental health issues, such as depression or anxiety, can be identified through changes in behavior, mood, thinking patterns, physical appearance, or everyday functioning. If any of these are noticed it is recommended that professional assistance be sought right away.

There are a number of treatments and resources available to help manage mental health conditions, including therapy and medication. It is important for women to discuss their treatment options with their doctor or other healthcare provider in order to select the best option for them. Additionally, self-care activities such as exercise, yoga, mindfulness, journaling, and spending time with friends can be used to promote emotional well-being.

It is essential that women have the resources and support they need to maintain their mental health. Mental health awareness campaigns, community outreach programs, and educational initiatives can all help raise awareness of the importance of emotional well-being and provide access to resources that may be beneficial for those struggling with mental illness. Through these efforts, we can work to create an environment of understanding and acceptance that allows women to seek the help they need.

It is also important to recognize the role of social determinants in mental health outcomes for women. Factors such as poverty, gender-based violence, access to healthcare, or discrimination can all have a powerful impact on their emotional well-being. By providing support for these issues, we can create a more equitable society that is better equipped to meet the needs of everyone.

Overall, women's mental health is an important issue that deserves attention and support from all sectors of society. With the right resources and education, we can work together to ensure that all women have access to the care they need to lead healthy and fulfilling lives.

Through research, advocacy, and policy changes, we can also work to reduce the stigma associated with mental health issues and create an environment that is more conducive to seeking help when needed. By taking a holistic approach to women's mental health, we can help ensure that everyone has access to the resources they need for long-term emotional well-being.

In addition, it is important to provide access to emotional support services and counseling. Women's mental health can benefit from having a safe space to explore their emotions and feelings, and gain insight into their own mental health needs. This can help them to develop greater understanding of themselves and make informed decisions about the care they need for optimal emotional well-being.

Finally, it is crucial to promote self-care practices that support emotional well-being. Taking time for oneself and engaging in activities like yoga or meditation can be beneficial for mental health. Making sure one takes the time to rest and relax is also important for overall wellbeing, as well as eating healthily and exercising regularly. By promoting healthy habits, we can create a more positive environment for women's mental health.

By investing in the necessary resources and education, we can ensure that all women have access to the care they need to lead healthy and fulfilling lives. Through support services, therapy, and self-care practices, we can create a healthier culture around mental health and make sure everyone has the opportunity to reach their fullest potential.

Chapter 7.1 Recognizing Signs of Emotional Distress

Recognizing the signs of emotional distress in women is crucial for timely intervention and support. Common signs include a persistent state of sadness, anxiety, or emptiness, accompanied by mood swings that may range from extreme happiness to intense depression. You may also notice a change in sleeping patterns, such as insomnia or excessive sleeping. Other indicators can involve a shift in appetite and weight, withdrawal from social activities, and a decline in performance at work or school. More severe signs encompass thoughts about death or suicide, severe restlessness, and engaging in risky behaviors. It's important to remember that these signs can vary among individuals, and professional help should be sought if emotional distress is suspected.

If you or someone you know is exhibiting any of the signs mentioned above, it's important to seek help. Mental health professionals can offer guidance and support with managing emotions and addressing underlying issues. With the right treatment, individuals can learn strategies for self-care and develop a healthier outlook on life. It's never too late to start the journey towards improved mental well-being. By taking the initiative to support yourself and others, we can ensure a brighter future for all.

It's also important to remember that there is no one-size-fits-all solution for emotional distress. Everyone's unique situation requires specialized care and attention. There are a variety of available interventions, including medication, therapy, lifestyle changes, and support groups. Taking the time to find the right approach can make all the difference in restoring your mental health and overall wellbeing.

At the end of the day, emotional distress doesn't have to be a life sentence. With the right resources and support, individuals can reclaim their lives for themselves and start on a path towards healing. Taking that first step is key – so don't wait any longer to get help. You deserve to live a life of joy and fulfillment, no matter what life throws your way. We all have the power to navigate our emotions and build a better tomorrow for ourselves and those around us.

No matter how hard things may seem, remember that there is always hope in difficult times. You are not alone in your journey – seek out resources, reach out to trusted friends and family members, and above all else, be kind to yourself. With a bit of determination and the right support, you can reclaim your mental health and create a healthier future for yourself. It's never too late to start on the path towards healing.

So don't hesitate to take action today. Reach out for help, make meaningful connections with those around you, and above all else, remember that you are strong and capable of overcoming anything. Through both the good times and bad, you have the power within you to make your life a masterpiece.

Let's take a stand against emotional distress today, and together we can create a brighter future for ourselves and those around us. With determination, resilience, and faith in our own strength, there is nothing that we cannot overcome.

Let's be the change we want to see in the world, and together we can create a more vibrant, joyful future for us all. Together is the key – so don't wait any longer to seek help, make meaningful connections with those around you, and never forget that you are strong enough to overcome anything life throws your way. You deserve to live a life of joy and fulfillment, no matter what the odds may be.

Take a stand against emotional distress today – together we can create a brighter future for ourselves and those around us. Let's be the change we want to see in the world, and never forget that we all have the power within us to make our lives into masterpieces. With determination and resilience, anything is possible.

Let's further spread this message of hope and support to everyone around us. Let's start conversations with our friends and family about mental health, and make sure that no one ever feels alone or ashamed for struggling with emotional distress. We can all be a part of the movement to create a brighter future, one conversation at a time.

We all have the power to break down stigmas and make sure that no one ever feels ashamed for asking for help or taking care of their mental health. Together, let's strive to create an environment where everyone feels welcome to seek out help and express themselves authentically without judgement.

So here's to a brighter future – one full of hope, resilience, and unconditional love. Let's make our lives into something beautiful together.

Chapter 7.2 Supporting Her Mental Health Journey

Embarking on a mental health journey is a significant step towards achieving overall wellbeing. It's a path that requires understanding, compassion, and consistent support. Be there for her by listening attentively and without judgment when she shares her feelings. Encourage her to seek professional help if needed and assure her that there's no shame in reaching out. Remind her that taking care of mental health is just as important as physical health and that every step she takes, however small, is progress. It's essential to reinforce that her journey is personal, and it's okay to move at her own pace. Most women grow in strength when they know they have someone to lean on. So don't forget to be a source of comfort and security as she learns to manage her mental health.

It's also important to create an environment that promotes self-care, routine, and structure. This will give her the space she needs to practice positive habits like getting enough sleep, eating healthily, and exercising. Being mindful of her stressors and triggers can help her find balance in the midst of chaos. Of course, recovery is not a linear journey that leads to an endpoint. It's something that requires continual self-care and self-reflection. As such, it's important to provide ongoing support throughout the entire process—whether she's feeling good or bad. Offer your help in any way you can, but be mindful of respecting her boundaries and autonomy as well.

At the end of the day, being there for someone on their mental health journey is not only a privilege, it's also an opportunity to witness true strength and courage. Encourage her to keep going and remind her how much of a difference she's making in her life and the lives of others. By providing support and showing compassion, you can help her reach new heights on her journey to recovery. Mental health is an ongoing conversation, never forget to let your loved ones know that you're always here for them. Let them know they are not alone in this journey, and you will be with her through the highs and lows. Supporting someone's mental health requires patience, understanding, and sometimes a little bit of humour. Above all else, remind them to take care of themselves first—and that it's okay to reach out for help when they need it. Remember that everyone has their own unique needs and preferences when it comes to seeking help. Some people may prefer professional support such as talking to a therapist, while others may find comfort in spending time with a close friend or family member. It's important to be flexible and open-minded when it comes to providing the kind of support she needs on her mental health journey.

It can take courage to ask for help, so make sure you encourage your loved one to take the first step and reach out when they're feeling down. Show them that you are there for them, no matter what, and remind them to never give up on themselves. With the right kind of support, anything is possible.

Sometimes it might not seem like it, but we all have within us the strength and resilience to make it through difficult times. We all have our own unique capacity to cope with life's challenges. So the next time your loved one is struggling with their mental health, offer words of hope and encouragement. Let them know that they can find strength in even the smallest things—a sunny day, a walk in nature, a funny movie—and encourage them to take it one step at a time. Make sure to check in regularly with your loved one and ask how they're doing. A simple text message, phone call or visit can mean the world to someone who is struggling with their mental health. Ask them what they need from you—and if there's anything else you can do to help. Most importantly, be there to listen without judgement.

It's important to remember that mental health is just as important as physical health. As a friend or family member, you have the power to be a source of hope and light in your loved one's life—and help them get the care they need and deserve. No matter what, always make sure your loved one knows that you are there for them. And remind them to never give up on their own journey of mental health and wellbeing. Together, you can help make a positive difference in their life.

If things get too difficult, don't hesitate to reach out for professional help – it might just be the best decision you ever made. Mental health services like therapists, psychologists, and counselors can provide invaluable support when it comes to helping your loved one cope with their mental health issues. So don't be afraid to make that call or appointment if the situation calls for it. At the end of the day, mental health is a journey—and we all need someone to talk to along the way. Show your loved one you care by offering your help, understanding, and support. Together you can make a big difference in their mental health journey.

Remember—you are not alone! Reach out for help if you're feeling overwhelmed. There are so many resources available, from hotlines to online support groups.

Chapter 7.3 Seeking Professional Help when Needed

It's crucial to acknowledge when professional help is needed and have the courage to seek it out. Whether it's a physical health issue, a mental health concern, or a legal matter, getting assistance from a qualified professional can make a significant difference. They have the training and expertise to provide guidance, support, and treatment. Remember, asking for help isn't a sign of weakness; it's a step towards resolution and improved well-being.

Taking the time to research the right person or organization for your needs can feel overwhelming and intimidating. However, having a clear plan of action will help make the process smoother. Make sure to ask questions, read reviews, and trust your instincts when it comes to finding the best professional for the job! Ultimately, having an advocate in your corner can be invaluable. Don't hesitate to reach out today. You don't have to go through it alone.

When seeking help, the most important thing is communication. Openly sharing your concerns and expectations with a professional can make all the difference in finding success. Be sure to be honest and provide as much detail as possible regarding your situation, so that you can get the best advice tailored specifically for you. Don't be afraid to ask questions and voice any hesitations or worries you may have; a good professional will take the time to answer them.

Though it can feel intimidating, asking for help is often the most empowering choice. Seeking out support from qualified professionals can be an invaluable way to start your journey towards improved well-being. Take the time to research the right person or organization for your needs and trust your instincts; having an advocate in your corner can be invaluable. Don't hesitate to reach out today and get the help you need!

If you're unsure what kind of professional you should consult, it may be beneficial to start with a primary care doctor or mental health provider. They can assess your needs and provide referrals to specialists if needed. Your primary care doctor can also connect you with support groups and other community organizations to help get the resources that are right for you.

At the same time, don't be afraid to seek out help from trusted friends or family members. Talking openly about your struggles with someone who knows you well can be a great source of comfort and understanding. Though they may not have professional expertise, they will likely provide an open ear and kind support to help you through your difficulties.

No matter what path you take, don't forget that seeking help is a sign of strength and self-care. It takes courage to face your own challenges and it's worth investing the time and energy to find the best solutions for you. With a little hard work and dedication, you can start feeling better soon!

Remember that there are plenty of options available to help with any mental health issue. Whether it's seeing a therapist, joining an online support group, or talking to your primary care doctor, seeking outside counseling and support is an important step in taking care of yourself. Taking the time to find the right professional for your needs can make all the difference, so don't hesitate to reach out today!

Finding a sense of peace and balance is possible, no matter how difficult things may feel. With a little help and guidance, you can start working towards improving your emotional health and wellbeing. You deserve to feel your best, so don't be afraid to take the first step on your journey towards healing.

Good luck and take care!

If you or someone you know needs help now, please call the National Suicide Prevention Lifeline at 1-800-273-TALK (8255). This free service is available 24 hours a day, 7 days a week. If you are in an emergency situation, call 911 immediately.

The Substance Abuse and Mental Health Services Administration (SAMHSA) also provides a 24-hour toll-free confidential treatment referral service that can connect you with the help you need, no matter where you are in the United States. You can call this number at 1-800-662-HELP (4357).

If you're outside of the United States, you can find a list of international mental health resources here: https://www.who.int/mental_health/en/.

No matter what your current situation is, there are people who care and who want to help. All it takes is a bit of courage to start the conversation and get the assistance you need. You deserve to be happy and healthy, and asking for help is the first step in making that happen.

We hope these resources will encourage you to take the leap and seek out the support you need! Remember that it's okay to ask for help, and it's important to take care of yourself.

Stay strong!

Chapter 8 Empathizing with Her Life Experiences

Her life experiences have been a testament to resilience and courage. Each step she took, each decision made, was a reflection of her strength and determination. Despite the adversities and challenges, she held her ground, fueling her journey with sheer will and an unyielding spirit. We can't help but empathize with her; her life narrative is not just a personal story; it is a lesson in tenacity and perseverance for all of us.

We must look to her life as an example of what it means to stay true to oneself in the face of adversity and strive for success no matter the odds. Her story serves as a reminder that we should never give up on our dreams, no matter how hard they may seem. She has shown us that with dedication and determination, we can achieve anything. Let us all remember her and the unyielding spirit she embodied.

That same strength of spirit can be found in our daily lives, if we take the time to identify it within ourselves and others. It is up to us to recognize these inspiring qualities and use them as motivation for doing great things. Whether you are facing a challenge or celebrating a success, let us all remember the unyielding spirit of the brave and courageous. Let us use it to push ourselves forward into a brighter future. Together, we can create a world that supports and encourages everyone to reach their full potential.

Let us honor her life by embodying the same strength of character she displayed and committing ourselves to never giving up on our dreams. We can all aspire to be as brave and determined as she was, and in doing so, carry her legacy forward. Let us embrace the unyielding spirit of her life and use it to overcome all obstacles, reach our goals, and create a better future for ourselves. Together we can make this world a place where everyone is empowered to pursue their dreams with courage and resilience.

Let us set an example of what it means to stay true to oneself and never give up on the things that matter. With this unyielding spirit, we can create a better tomorrow for ourselves and generations to come.

We are all capable of achieving great things if we just believe in ourselves and never lose sight of our dreams. If we stay true to our values and remain dedicated to our goals, there is no limit to what we can achieve. Let us all follow the example of the brave and courageous, and never let adversity stand in our way; together, we can create a better tomorrow!

That's why it's important to keep striving for greatness. No matter what challenge life throws our way, never give up on yourself. Keep pushing forward and remember the unyielding spirit of those who have come before us. With courage and resilience, we can create a brighter future for all.

Let's all remember to stay dedicated, determined, and driven in the pursuit of our dreams. No matter what life throws at us, let us remain true to ourselves and never give up. Remember the unyielding spirit of those who have come before us and use it to fight for a better tomorrow. Together, we can create a world that is fairer, brighter, and more prosperous for everyone.

Onward we go—with courage in our hearts and the unyielding spirit of those who have come before us. Let's create a better future together!

That's why it's important to stay connected and keep our spirits high. Reach out to friends, family, and those who share your values for support and encouragement. The more we share in the journey, the stronger we can become—together!

Let's never forget that with strength, courage, and ambition—we can build a brighter tomorrow. Let's use our unyielding spirit to create a better world for ourselves and generations to come. Believe in yourself, stay true to your values, and never give up on your dreams! Together, we can make a difference. Onward!

Let us take the time to appreciate the unyielding spirit of those who have come before us and to continue their legacy. By passing down our values, ideas, and dreams to future generations, we can ensure that a brighter future for all remains possible. Let's not forget that only with hard work, dedication, and resilience can we create a better tomorrow. So let us never give up hope and always stay true to ourselves and our dreams.

The unyielding spirit of those who have come before us is a powerful force for positive change. Let's strive to carry on our legacy by dedicating ourselves to the pursuit of a brighter tomorrow. We can create a world where everyone has the opportunity to reach their potential, achieve success, and live according to their values.

Chapter 8.1 Understanding Her Past and Its Impact

When two individuals decide to enter into a romantic relationship, they bring their entire selves to the table. That includes their upbringing, childhood experiences, and past relationships. For many, the past may seem like a separate entity from the present, but it's important to recognize that it has a significant impact on our behavior, emotions, and decisions. This is particularly true for women, who are often affected by past traumas, abuses, and neglect. In this blog post, we are going to explore the importance of understanding her past and its impact on the present. We'll be offering tips for men and women to help them navigate this aspect of a relationship.

1. Listen Without Judgment: One of the most important things you can do is listen to her stories and experiences without judgment or criticism. This may be difficult if her past involves things that are uncomfortable or difficult to hear, but it's important to understand that this is her reality and it's shaped who she is today. Rather than shutting down or becoming defensive, try to be open-minded and empathetic.

2. Respect Her Boundaries: When a person has experienced trauma or abuse in the past, they may struggle with trust and intimacy. It's important to respect her boundaries and not push her into anything she's not comfortable with. If physical intimacy is a struggle, take things slow and let her set the pace. If she needs space, give her the time and respect she needs.

3. Seek Professional Help: If her past is particularly traumatic and impacts her daily life, encourage her to seek professional help. Therapy can be incredibly helpful for processing past traumas and developing coping mechanisms. You can offer to provide support and even attend therapy sessions together if she's open to it.

4. Educate Yourself: Take the time to educate yourself about trauma, abuse, and their impact on individuals. This will not only help you understand her better, but it will also help you support her in the best way possible. Attend workshops or read books on these topics to gain more insight and knowledge.

5. Communicate Openly: Communication is key in any relationship, but it's even more important when dealing with past traumas. Encourage her to communicate openly about her thoughts and feelings and be willing to do the same. By having open and honest communication, you'll be able to address issues before they become bigger problems.

Understanding her past and its impact is essential for building a healthy and fulfilling relationship. It requires empathy, patience, and open-mindedness, but the benefits are immense. When we take the time to understand and support our partners, we grow together and build deeper connections. By listening without judgment, respecting her boundaries, seeking professional help, educating ourselves, and communicating openly, we can create a safe and loving environment for both partners. Remember, she is not defined by her past, but it has influenced who she is today. Show her the care and support she deserves, and the relationship will benefit her in more ways than one.

Chapter 8.2 Supporting Her Through Challenges

When supporting her through challenges, it's essential to be a good listener first. Allow her to express her feelings and thoughts without interruption, judgement or unnecessary advice. Be patient and understanding, realizing that everyone deals with adversity in their own unique way. Encourage her to see challenges as opportunities for growth and learning, rather than as insurmountable obstacles. Offer help when needed, but also give her the space to solve problems on her own. This can empower her and boost her confidence. Lastly, always remind her of her strengths and past achievements to inspire resilience and perseverance. With your support, she can overcome anything.

When celebrating her successes, make sure to express genuine enthusiasm and admiration for her accomplishments. Be creative when you congratulate her; a simple text message or verbal expression of appreciation will only go so far! Pull out all the stops for special occasions—surprise and delight her with a heartfelt gesture like flowers or a handwritten card. Or, go the extra mile and plan an unforgettable experience that celebrates her successes in a unique way. No matter how you choose to celebrate her wins, make sure she feels your admiration and respect for all that she has achieved.

At the end of the day, it's important to remember that true support is more than just words—it's the little actions that go a long way in showing her you care. Make sure to demonstrate your dedication and loyalty by keeping your promises, being dependable in times of need, and offering a listening ear whenever she needs. Be there for her as an advocate, mentor, friend and cheerleader—that's what true supportive listening is all about!

Giving her a safe space to express herself is also key—create an environment where she can freely and openly share her thoughts without fear of judgement. Encourage her to talk about both the successes and disappointments in her life, and always remember that it's not your job to fix things for her. The best thing you can do is simply listen and offer a kind word of encouragement when appropriate.

No matter how far along she is in her journey, your presence and support will make all the difference. Help her stay focused on her goahelp her get back up when she falls down—supportive listening is about being there for someone through both the highs and lows of life. Show your appreciation for her and all she has accomplished by being a supportive listener. She'll thank you for it!

When the going gets tough, be sure to remind her of all her successes—share stories, remember moments and celebrate milestones together. Whether it's a simple pat on the back or an elaborate night out, take time to recognize how far she's come and the progress she has made. Use these moments to reiterate your support and willingness to listen, no matter what the situation may be.

Above all, make sure that she knows you'll always have her back—because when it comes down to it, only a true friend will be there with supportive listening every step of the way. So never forget to be that friend, and your friendship will only grow stronger for it.

Being a supportive listener isn't always easy—it takes time, energy and effort. But the rewards are well worth it. Not only can you strengthen your bond with her, but you also get to witness firsthand all the wonderful things she is capable of achieving. Be the best listener you can be and watch her thrive. It's sure to make your friendship stronger and even more beautiful than before.

Chapter 8.3 Celebrating Her Triumphs

In the realm of her accomplishments, each triumph stands as a testament to her relentless hard work, resilience, and unwavering determination. These victories, whether large or small, are not mere marks of success, but milestones in her journey, each one shaping her into the strong, confident individual she is today. So, let's take a moment to acknowledge these triumphs, to applaud her fortitude and to celebrate the inspiring journey she has embarked upon.

At the end of every grueling climb is a breathtaking view, one that reminds her how far she has come and what's still possible. Every setback simply serves as another steppingstone to success and each victory brings with it an even greater hunger for more. She understands that on this journey, there are no shortcuts - only hard work and perseverance lead to enduring success.

And yet, even when the obstacles seem insurmountable, she never gives up. She stays focused on her goals and takes each setback in her stride, determined to come out stronger on the other end. Her unwavering courage is a source of inspiration for those who witness her ascent and reminds them that anything is possible with hard work and dedication.

Today, her triumphant journey continues, and she is constantly striving to reach new heights. She remains a beacon of hope and courage for us all. Let us applaud her efforts, celebrate her successes, and be inspired by the example she has set on this remarkable journey.

This is but the beginning of what will surely become an inspiring legacy. The story of her triumph is one that will live on for many generations to come. Here's to her courageous journey and the legacy she continues to build!

May she continue to reach new heights with each passing day, staying determined, resilient, and never losing sight of her dreams. Cheers to an amazing individual who has done so much in such a short amount of time. Let's all take a moment to recognize this remarkable journey she is on and the lessons it teaches us.

No matter how hard life may get, if you stay focused on your goals and never give up, you too can make that triumphant climb! Thank you for inspiring us all with your courage and strength. Here's to a bright future!

May our paths cross and we continue to support each other on our own journeys of success, dreaming big and never giving up. We have all the resources within us to reach new heights, so let's use them and keep powering forward! Here's to inspiring individuals, such as her, who serve as a reminder that anything is possible with hard work, dedication, and resilience.

Let us never forget the trials, tribulations and successes she experienced on her journey, as they were instrumental in paving the way for a new era of success. Let's raise our glasses to an amazing individual whose courage has created a path that we can all follow! Long may her triumphant journey continue!

May this journey of success serve as a reminder to us all that no obstacles are too big, and no dream is too small. With the right tools, passion and determination, we can all reach our goals, one milestone at a time. Here's to her incredible legacy and many more to come!

So here's to you and your dreams, may we one day be able to look back on your journeys with the same pride and accomplishment. May we all find strength in difficult times, while continuing to strive for greatness. Let's keep pushing forward no matter how hard it gets and, just like her, never give up on achieving our goals!

May you all continue to be inspired, take action and work hard to make our dreams come true. With each of us taking a step towards success every day, together we will push forward to become the best versions of ourselves. Here's to the journey ahead - may it lead us all closer to our goals!

And finally, may we take this journey together and support each other in our individual pursuits of success. By doing so, we will be able to create a future where success knows no bounds!

Let's raise a glass to celebrate the successes achieved thus far, as well as those yet to come. For every success, there will be a moment of triumph – something to be proud of. Here's to the journey and the countless moments of glory!

Conclusion

In conclusion, loving a woman involves much more than just expressing feelings. It requires patience, understanding, and communication. It's about respecting her individuality, supporting her ambitions, and celebrating her accomplishments. Love is also expressed through acts of kindness, being there for her in times of need, and showing genuine interest in her thoughts and feelings. A healthy and loving relationship is built on mutual respect, trust, and a shared commitment to growth and happiness.

With love, comes understanding and appreciation for the person you are with, as well as a desire to make them feel cherished. By cultivating these qualities in your relationship, you can develop a deep connection that will last through both good times and bad.

No matter how strong your feelings are, it's important to remember that a loving relationship requires effort from both parties. Both partners must be willing to learn about each other, compromise when necessary, and resolve conflicts with respect. It's also important to keep communication lines open and express gratitude when it is deserved. Through these practices, your relationship can evolve into a deeper level of understanding and love.

Ultimately, loving someone means seeing them for who they really are - flaws and all - and choosing to accept them unconditionally. It is a powerful emotion that can bring two people together, creating an environment of growth, mutual understanding, and joy. Investing in your relationship with patience and persistence will ensure that it stands the test of time and becomes something truly special.

At the end of the day, love is a beautiful thing - not just between couples, but among friends and family as well. Acknowledging its power and presence in your life can help you create meaningful relationships that bring joy and fulfillment to everyone involved. Loving women is a beautiful, worthwhile endeavor, and one that you should cherish for years to come.

Don't miss out!

Visit the website below and you can sign up to receive emails whenever Calvin Brown Sr. publishes a new book. There's no charge and no obligation.

https://books2read.com/r/B-A-VSTAB-APUOC

Connecting independent readers to independent writers.